Creative W:

vol 1 & 2

Amanda J Harrington

1

Creative Writing for Kids vol 1 & 2

First edition copyright © Amanda J. Harrington, 2013

New edition copyright © Amanda J. Harrington, 2015

Cover created using original images by © Sergey Khakimullin | Dreamstime.com and © Alexandra Petruk | Dreamstime.com

978-1-291-37328-8

www.amandajharrington.co.uk

2

Contents

4

Introduction

All too often, children are put off creative writing by feeling they have to do it *right*. I want to help children enjoy writing their own stories. Creativity comes in lots of different packages, and not just the ones marked with a red tick or a gold star!

This book comes from original exercises and activities created especially for one-to-one lessons, creative writing groups, school visits and for my own children when they were home educated. The focus is on fun and creative thinking, so that literacy and writing skills happen more naturally without it feeling like work.

The age range for all the books in the Creative Writing for Kids range is 7-14, depending on ability. Lots of exercises can be expanded to suit keen writers and many have been written for reluctant learners and special needs students.

How to Use this Book

When working through the book, children should only be thinking about their stories or poems. I have deliberately left out any mention of spelling, punctuation, grammar and other technical matters. This book is about enjoying creativity and freeing children so that they are not afraid to try new things and attempt more challenging work.

The exercises are for a variety of ages and abilities, but can all be adapted to suit individual children. I have known children who could barely write who created wonderful stories through pictures and conversations, using these exercises. Confident writers can adapt the work to suit themselves and expand from it as much as they like.

The exercises can be completed in any order and there are linked themes, such as free story-telling or poetry, throughout the book.

Draw and Write: Favourite Place

Draw a picture of your favourite place. This can be somewhere you like to go, or a place you have never been but would love to visit.

Now describe the place in words, using the picture to help you. Imagine you have to answer questions about it, as if you are describing it to someone who has never been there before.

Look at the next page for some ideas to help you.

Think about:

1. Where is it?

2. What kind of place is it?

3. Who goes there with you?

4. Why do you like it so much?

Example

My favourite place is the farm because I can help with the animals and play with my Gran's dog, Caspar. The farm is big, with lots of fields and has sheep and 2 horses.

A Story in Pictures: The Scary Path

You are going to make a story, using only pictures. In this story, you are walking along a path and you are afraid.

Using pictures drawn by yourself, cut from a book or printed from a computer, show your journey along the scary path.

You can add titles, but otherwise your pictures must tell the story.

Jumble Words: Mrs Fickle

Mrs Fickle has opened a new shop. So far, we know nothing about Mrs Fickle or her shop.

Look at the words below. Choose **at least 3** from each list, then write a short story describing Mrs Fickle and her shop.

You can also draw pictures, using the words you have chosen to help you.

Mrs Fickle

Jolly, clever, tall, fat, freckle, hat, stern, giggles, grey, ginger, red, old, loud, friendly, cold, young, pretty, cat, curly, fussy, sleepy.

Her Shop

Small, smelly, sweets, flowers, counter, soap, vegetables, fresh, paintings, big, empty, books, paper, toys, games, clothes, food.

Tell the Tale: Away We Go!

Look at the picture and think of a story to match it. If you have an idea, just try to write about it.

If you need some extra help:

1. How do you think the girl is feeling?

2. Where do you think she is going?

3. How did she learn how to fly?

Story Practice: A Beary Short Tail

You are a brown bear called Fudge and you live in a cave on the edge of the forest. One day, you catch a hunter and use a People spell. Instantly, you have swapped places with the hunter.

You look like a man but inside you're still a bear. You tie up the hunter at the back of the cave and set off for town.

Now write about what happens when you get there.

Comic Strip: Otto Loves TV

Make a story in a comic strip. You can make it as long or as short as you like, but there are three things you need to know to help you:

1. Otto loves TV!

2. Otto loves swimming.

3. Otto likes experimenting.

Freestyle: Good Times

Here are some ideas for you to use in a story or a poem. Make your story or poem as long or as short as you like.

You can decide what happens in it and who your characters are.

Just choose one of the ideas and have a go.

1. A tree covered in lights.

2. A trip to the beach.

3. A table full of chocolate eggs.

4. A candle-lit pumpkin.

5. A present with your name on it.

6. Going on holiday.

7. A giant jar full of pennies.

8. Having a party.

9. Getting a little brother or sister.

10. A water slide on a hot day.

Double Act: Runn-ing

You are going to write a story, but there are two things you need to include in it.

One is that there must be lots of **movement** in the story.

The other is that at least 7 words must end in the '**ing**' sound. Have a go!

Tell the Tale: Peeking!

What kind of a story goes with this picture? It can be any kind of story you like, but think about:

1. How is the boy feeling?

2. Is he playing a game or really hiding?

3. Where is he hiding?

Adventures into the Unknown:

The Climb

Write a poem, using the three ideas below. You decide how long your poem should be and whether or not you want it to rhyme.

1. You are climbing over very hard ground

2. You almost fall.

3. You hear strange noises.

Remember!

A poem does not have to rhyme or be very long. Just have a go!

Freestyle: Scary Stuff

Here are some ideas for you to use in a story or a poem. Make your story or poem as long or as short as you like.

You can decide what happens in it and who your characters are.

Just choose one of the ideas and have a go.

1. A dark room.

2. Homework.

3. A spider's web in the corner.

4. A wasp's nest.

5. Educational television.

6. Falling out with your friends.

7. The Ghost Train.

8. Meeting new people.

9. A noise in the night.

10. Getting lost.

Jumble Words: Characters

Look at the words below. Choose some of them to create **two different people.**

For instance, you could choose 'Miss' and 'Egg' to create 'Miss Egg' as one of your characters.

Simon Lock Pippa Miss Jilly Anna Benjamin Jumbles Mr

Anthony Clover Mrs Penny Emma Carter Buttons Winter

Mortimer Pennyworth Bud Alfred Doctor Gray Harvest Jake

What are they like?

Write down the names of your two characters. Now answer these questions about them:

1. What colour hair do they have?

2. Are they friendly?

3. What is their favourite food?

4. Are they young or old?

5. Do they have a pet?

6. Do they live on their own?

Now you can draw pictures of your characters, to match your description.

After you have created your character, think of what kind of story you might see them in. You can either write the story, or describe what might happen in the story.

Story Words: Mixture

Look at the headings below and think of as many words as you can to go with each one. I have given you some words to get you started.

Then choose at least **two** words from each heading and put them into a story. You decide how long you want the story to be. Look at the examples to help you.

Colours: *red*

Weather: *sunny*

Animals: *leopard*

Feelings: *grumpy*

Example story (very short!): The grumpy leopard sat on the red sand, resting in the sunshine.

Story Practice: Princess Angelica

Angelica has always been the worst princess in the palace. One day she finds a spinning wheel in the attic and pricks her finger, hoping Prince Charming will come.

Instead, she opens the door and finds herself on the top floor of a modern shopping centre. She can go back, prick her finger and return to her own land, or carry on into this new world. What happens next?

Double Act: Sudden~ly

You are going to write a story, but there are two things you need to include in it.

One is that there must be a **surprise.**

The other is that at least 5 words in your story must end in the **'ly'** sound. Have a go!

Poster Perfect: Wanted!

Draw a picture of yourself or find a photo and stick it onto a piece of paper.

Next, imagine you are making a Wanted poster for a terrible villain - *you* are the villain!

There are two important things you need to include on your poster: the **crime** you committed and the **reward** for your capture. Everything else is up to you!

Comic Strip: Jenny's Foot

This story is going to be a comic strip, with a set of pictures and words to tell the story.

You don't need many words when you are using pictures, just a few to explain what is happening and speech bubbles if you want to show people talking.

Look at the sentences on the next page. They are in the wrong order. You need to rearrange them and then make a comic strip story around them.

Sentences

Her foot was twice as big as it should be.

Jenny's mother hated snails.

The shoes looked beautiful!

Jenny's friend, Claire, had very big feet.

She tiptoed across the garden.

"Oh no!" she cried.

Jenny loved shoes.

She had to hop all the way to the bathroom.

Claire loved football.

The snails didn't care

It was everywhere!

Adventures into the Unknown: The New Start

Write a poem, using the three ideas below. You decide how long your poem should be and whether or not you want it to rhyme.

If you like, you can write it as a tiny story, then turn it into a poem.

1. You have to go somewhere for the first time.

2. Everyone else seems happy.

3. Memories of how things used to be.

Tell the Tale: In the Snow!

Think of a story to go with this picture about being in the snow.

It can be any kind of story you like, as long as it matches the picture in some way.

Think about:

1. Some people love snow and some people hate it.

2. There is fake snow as well as the real thing!

3. You might have to travel to find proper snow.

Story Recipe: Your Story

You are the main character in this story, so write it in the **first person.** This means writing things like, 'I did' or 'I want to' and 'I felt' etc. The story can be as long or as short as you like.

As well as having **yourself** in the story, you need to include:

Next door's cat

A new friend

A hundred newspapers

Write a Letter: You're Famous!

You've been asked to write to your fans, telling them how you became famous and what your life is like.

Decide what you want to be famous for. Will you be a pop star, footballer, writer or something else?

Then write your letter, with as many details as possible about your life and what it is like to be you.

Adventures into the Unknown: The Puppy

Write a poem, using the three ideas below. You decide how long your poem should be and whether or not you want it to rhyme.

1. A really bad smell.

2. A half-eaten shoe.

3. Nibbles.

Story Practice: Mrs Wrinklebottom

Mrs Wrinklebottom is your neighbour and she hates you. She thinks you make too much noise and run about a lot, even if you sit quietly and say nothing! Mrs Wrinklebottom is a big, scary woman so you are too frightened to make friends with her.

One day, your mother sends you round with some cakes for Mrs Wrinklebottom. You sneak in and leave them on the kitchen table. On your way out, you see Mrs Wrinklebottom in her hall cupboard. She hasn't seen you. A mad moment takes you over and you shut the cupboard door and lock it. Just for a second you enjoy it, then she starts to hammer on the door.

"Let me out!" she booms. "I know who did this! Wait till your mother finds out!"

Now you daren't let her out. It's too scary to think what she might do if you open the door, but you can't leave her in there forever. What should you do?

Draw and Write: Look Around You

Draw a picture of what you see around you, right now. Put as much detail into it as you can.

Now describe what is around you in words.

Think about

What is near you?

Are there any people?

What do you like about where you are?

Where would you rather be?

Freestyle: Moving Around

Here are some ideas for you to use in a story or a poem. Make your story or poem as long or as short as you like.

You can decide what happens in it and who your characters are.

Just choose one of the ideas and have a go.

Ideas

1. A short journey.

2. When we moved house.

3. A broken down car.

4. A cat running across a meadow.

5. The wheelie bin rolling off down the street.

6. Smoke from a bonfire curling up into the sky.

7. An ant scurrying across a picnic cloth.

8. Getting onto an aeroplane.

9. A rowing boat.

10. When Jessica's bag fell out of the bus.

Story Recipe: A Day Out

You are the main character in this story, so write it in the **first person.** This means writing things like, 'I did' or 'I want to' and 'I felt' etc.

As well as having yourself in the story, you need to include:

An unexpected stop

A half-sucked sweet

A grass covered hill

A loud voice

Story Practice: The Magic Pocket

Part One

You are given a pair of jeans for your birthday. Every time you put your hand in your pocket, you find a ten pound note. The pocket is magical and will refill with money each time you empty it. What do you do?

You can draw pictures to tell your story as well as writing.

Part Two

It is Saturday morning. You wake up late, ready to have more fun with the money coming out of your magic pocket. That's when you realise your jeans have been put in the wash.

When they're dry, you put them on and look in the pocket. You find a very small potato. What happens next? Does the magic pocket still work? Or does it only make potatoes now?

Write the rest of the story or tell it in pictures.

Tell the Tale: Popping!

Think of the word 'popping' and write a story to go with it and this picture.

Think about:

1. Some people don't like balloons.

2. Does a party need to have balloons?

3. How does the little girl in the picture feel?

Draw and Write: Where I live

Draw a picture of your home. Now describe your home in words, using your picture to help you.

Think about:

Do you live in a house or a bungalow?

A boat or a castle?

In a caravan or a flat?

What colour is your front door?

Do you have a garden?

Double Act: Decorat-ed

You are going to write a story, but there are two things you need to include in it.

One is that your story must be about the **Christmas** season.

The other is that at least 7 words must end in the **'ed'** sound. Have a go!

Adventures into the Unknown: The Visit

Write a poem, using the three ideas below. You decide how long your poem should be and whether or not you want it to rhyme.

1. You have to visit someone.

2. You feel afraid.

3. You are surprised.

Story Practice: Professor Nibbles

Every time you pass the hutch, you hear strange noises but when you open the door you only see Nibbles the guinea pig, eating food.

One day, you decide to find out what is going on. Creeping quietly up to the hutch, you slowly open the door. Inside, Nibbles is hammering at some kind of machine that takes up most of the room.

Suddenly, Nibbles spots you. He pats the side of the hutch and the wood slides right round, taking the machine away into a hidden room. Even when you look behind the hutch you can't see where it has gone.

What happens next?

Write a Letter: Saying Sorry

You need to write a letter to someone, saying you're sorry.

You can decide what you have done and who you are apologising to.

You can also decide whether it is a good apology, or if you don't really mean it and only want to get out of trouble!

Don't forget to include details of what you did wrong.

Double Act: Swimm-er!

You are going to write a story, but there are two things you need to include in it.

One is that there must be **sporty** things in your story.

The other is that you should have at least 6 words ending in the 'er' sound. Have a go!

A Story in Pictures: A Royal Baby

You are going to make a story, using only pictures. In this story, a new prince or princess has been born into a magical kingdom.

Using pictures drawn by yourself, cut from a book or printed from a computer, tell the story of the new baby. You can add titles, but otherwise your pictures must tell the story.

Don't forget to use lots of shiny colours in this story, as a royal baby will be given presents of gold, silver and jewels.

Tell the Tale! Water Slide

Think of a water slide and write a story to go with it.

It can be any kind of story you like, as long as it includes the water slide.

Don't forget, it doesn't have to be a big slide in a pool; it could be a slide in your back garden, with a hose pipe running down it.

Story Practice: The Lizard

Your friend Klaus is going on holiday and he wants you to look after his pet lizard, Boris. The trouble is, your parents *never* let you have any pets in the house.

You end up sneaking Boris the lizard into the house in your sports bag. He seems quite happy in there, so you leave him in the bag until everyone has gone to bed.

In the darkened house you open the bag to take Boris out. But he isn't there!

You search your room and then try to search the rest of the house but there's no sign of Boris. What happens next?

Story Recipe: Gnomes, Bats and a Ring

You are the main character in this story, so write it in the **first person**. This means writing things like, 'I did' or 'I want to' and 'I felt' etc.

As well as having yourself in the story, you need to include:

a garden gnome coming to life

bats in the night

a diamond ring sparkling in the darkness

Poster Perfect: Guinea Pigs Galore!

Your guinea pigs have had babies. And the babies have had babies. It's reached the stage where you either need to find them new homes or move out and they can have the house to themselves.

Design a poster to advertise your guinea pigs. Make them sound as beautiful and friendly as you can, and include lots of pictures so that people will want to buy them.

Try not to tell any lies about your guinea pigs but do your best to make people want to give them homes.

Story Practice: Furry Trousers

You bring your pet rat, Archie, into school one day so you can show him to your friends.

Unfortunately, Archie escapes from your bag and and runs into the school kitchen. He eats some lovely, juicy, mysteriously sparkly berries in a golden basket. Once he's eaten them all, he comes back to find you.

As soon as you touch him, you start to grow fur. Nice, soft, grey fur, like Archie's. Before you know it, you're covered in fur and can only squeak. You look down at Archie, to see if he's okay.

'Gosh! This is exciting!' he says, grinning up at you.

What happens next?

Tell the tale: Topsy-turvy!

Oh dear! Everything seems to have been turned upside down. Or is it you that is the wrong way up?

Write a story based on this picture. You can make it about yourself or someone else.

Think about:

1. How did this happen?

2. Is it exciting or scary?

3. What could you do if you could walk on ceilings and up walls?

4. What happens if you can't control it?

5. And what could go wrong?

Story Recipe: Mysteries

You are the main character in this story, so write it in the **first person.** This means writing things like, 'I did' or 'I want to' and 'I felt' etc.

As well as having yourself in the story, you need to include:

A locked cupboard

An open book

A hidden secret

Adventures into the Unknown: The Boat Trip

Write a poem, using the three ideas below. You decide how long your poem should be and whether or not you want it to rhyme.

1. Life jackets.

2. A gust of wind.

3. The mist whispering around your face.

Tell the Tale: Merry Christmas!

Write a story about this little girl and her Christmas. Will something exciting happen?

Think about:

1. How does the little girl feel?

2. Is she having a good day?

3. Do you think she got what she wanted for Christmas?

Poster Perfect: Any Old Thing

You need to make some money, and fast, but the only thing you have to sell is an old coat. It has holes in the pockets and two buttons left. There is a hole in the back too.

Make a poster to sell the old coat. You can draw pictures, cut some out from books or print them out from a computer. The main thing is, you must make this poor old coat seem so **wonderful** that people can't resist it.

See what you can think of to make it seem fabulous!

Don't forget to describe the coat and tell people how much it costs.

Double Act: Butter-y

You are going to write a story, but there are two things you need to include in it.

One is that there must be **food** in your story.

The other is that at least 5 words must end in the 'y' sound. Have a go!

Tell the Tale: I'm not going to!

Write a story about this picture, including as many describing words as you can.

Think about:

1. What time of year is it?

2. Do you think the little girl is grumpy or enjoying herself?

3. What do you think happened to make her pull a face?

A Story in Pictures: A Little Visitor

You are going to make a story, using only pictures. In this story, your little cousin Derek has come to visit. He is only two and loves to run around, playing with things. He often breaks what he plays with.

Using pictures drawn by yourself, cut from a book or printed from a computer, tell the story of his visit. You can add titles, but otherwise your pictures must tell the story.

Write a Letter: A New Pen Pal

You are writing to someone who lives far away from you. This is the first letter you have ever sent them, so you need to tell them all about yourself.

Include what you like to do, where you live and anything else you think they need to know.

Don't forget to ask them about themselves. If you are going to be pen pals, you need to be interested in their life too.

Story Recipe: Four Legs and Feelings

You are the main character in this story, so write it in the **first person**. This means writing things like, 'I did' or 'I want to' and 'I felt' etc.

As well as having yourself in the story, you need to include:

a friendly goat

an angry sheep

a greedy little dog

Story Practice: A Woolly Jumper

Auntie Peggy has spent weeks knitting you a lovely new jumper. She knows you like colourful things so she used every spare ball of wool she had and mixed them together. Secretly, you hate your new jumper because it makes you look like a giant sweet but you promise to wear it every time Auntie Peggy visits.

Today Auntie Peggy is coming for lunch. You put on the jumper and take your dog for a walk. Then you wriggle under your bed looking for a game you lost. After that, you play chase with the dog in your garden.

As Auntie Peggy arrives, you look out at the back garden. There is something trailing all over the grass, and on the trees. It's something multi-coloured…

With a sinking heart, you look down at your jumper and see it is only half there. The other half is tangled round everything in the back garden. Even the dog has a bright woolly tail!

With only seconds to spare before Auntie Peggy walks in, what will you do?

Double Act: Happi-ness

You are going to write a story, but there are two things you need to include in it.

One is that there must be a lot of **feelings** in your story (you can choose more than one emotion).

The other is that at least 4 words must end in the **'ness'** sound. Have a go!

Tell the Tale: I don't know!

Look at this picture of a boy surrounded by sums and puzzles. Write a story about him and what is happening in the picture.

Think about:

1. Is he happy?

2. What do you think will happen next?

3. Would you like to be the boy?

Story Recipe: Time Out

You are the main character in this story, so write it in the **first person.** This means writing things like, 'I did' or 'I want to' and 'I felt' etc.

As well as having yourself in the story, you need to include:

your favourite game

TV on loud

playing on the beach

relaxing in your room

A Story in Pictures: The Holiday

You are going to make a story, using only pictures. In this story, you are going on holiday.

Using pictures drawn by yourself, cut from a book or printed from a computer, tell the story of your holiday. You can add titles, but otherwise your pictures must tell the story.

You can tell the story of a real holiday you have been on, or you can make up an imaginary holiday, where anything can happen.

Jumble Words: Diary of a Bad Week

You are filling in your diary. Look at the jumbled sentences and decide which day of the week they should be.

You can also draw pictures to decorate your week.

Days: Sunday Monday Tuesday Wednesday Thursday Friday Saturday

1. The handle fell off the bathroom door and I was stuck in there for an hour. I was late for school.

2. My cat was sick on my homework but the teacher thought it was me.

3. My little brother thinks worms are great and when I got home from school he had made them a home in my moneybox.

4. My mother wants us to eat healthy food. This is the third day I've had pineapple chunks in my lunch box.

5. The TV broke and I had to spend the morning doing my homework.

6. I was ill after eating too many pineapple chunks and had to stay

off school. Brilliant!

7. I opened my school bag in the middle of class and found my little brother had put the cat in there again. It took three teachers and a dinner lady to catch it.

Freestyle: Good Little Things

Here are some ideas for you to use in a story or a poem. Make your story or poem as long or as short as you like.

You can decide what happens in it and who your characters are.

Just choose one of the ideas and have a go.

1. A sledge on the snow.

2. Birthday cards with money in them.

3. A new packet of sweets.

4. A holiday full of sunshine.

5. Knowing how to work a DVD player.

6. My dog can answer the phone.

7. Breakfast in bed.

8. A trip to the toy shop.

9. My cat can catch spiders.

10. Glow-in-the-dark moon and stars.

Tell the Tale: Cabbages!

That is a very big cabbage! Write a story about the little girl and the giant cabbage.

Think about:

1. Is it a real cabbage?

2. How did she get there?

3. Does she like cabbages?

Story Recipe: Loved Things

You are the main character in this story, so write it in the **first person.** This means writing things like, 'I did' or 'I want to' and 'I felt' etc.

As well as having yourself in the story, you need to include:

a well-loved book

a golden key

a favourite thing

Draw and Write: Your Birthday

Draw a picture of your best birthday. This could be a picture of the presents, or the party, or even of you, enjoying yourself!

Now describe the birthday in words, using the picture to help you.

What made this birthday the best one? Was it the presents or the people around you?

What would your best present be, if you could have anything in the world?

Adventures into the Unknown: The Phone Box

Write a poem, using the three ideas below. You decide how long your poem should be and whether or not you want it to rhyme.

A lit phone box

An unexpected call

A new adventure

Story Recipe: The New Doll

You are the main character in this story, so write it in the **first person**. This means writing things like, 'I did' or 'I want to' and 'I felt' etc.

As well as having yourself in the story, you need to include:

A new doll

A sound in the corner

A little footstep

Freestyle: I'm a Hero!

Here are some ideas for you to use in a story or a poem. Make your story or poem as long or as short as you like.

You can decide what happens in it and who your characters are.

Just choose one of the ideas and have a go.

1. A great disguise

2. Jumping very high

3. A trusty sidekick

4. A quick-thinking friend

5. A magical item

6. Super strength

7. Where did she go?

8. A grand plan to take over the world

9. A shining cape.

10. I'm the hero!

Creative Writing for Kids vol 2

Story Practice: Sherlock

Last night you had a dream that your best friend Sherlock turned into a goose and flew away. When you go to school, you find out Sherlock has moved house suddenly and without saying goodbye.

You can't shake the feeling something is wrong. You don't believe he flew away, but you are worried about him. If he was moving house, he would have told you.

You go to his house and find a SOLD sign outside. Does that mean it was true? Would he really leave without telling you? Or is there something more sinister going on?

What happens next?

Comic Strip: Dragons have feelings too

Make a story in a comic strip. You can make it as long or as short as you like, but there are three things you need to know to help you:

Dragons are very bad-tempered

Dragons like to eat bacon

Dragons don't like to be laughed at

Looks familiar...super villain

You are going to write about someone you know and create a story just for them.

Turn the person you know into a **super villain**. Make sure they do lots of bad things and are definitely not the hero!

Do they become a better person by the end? Or do they steal a hot air balloon and escape into the mountains? Or vanish in their giant submarine, hiding at the bottom of the sea?

Story Starter: Mysterious Noises

All week you've been woken by strange noises coming from outside. As soon as you're awake, they stop. It's almost as if they know you're listening!

At first you try to ignore them but as the week goes on, you become more and more tired. You must find out what it is.

The next night, instead of going to bed, you wait in the darkness of the garden, hiding under a heavy blanket so no one can see you.

Using one or more of the ideas below, write about what happens next. It can be anything you like but you must include one of these ideas in a way that makes sense within the story.

Ideas

Broken torch

Rustling feet

A moving tail

Time to run

Calamity!

A story in pictures: When I was little

You are going to make a story, using only pictures.

In this story, you are going to talk about what you were like when you were little. Did you look completely different? What kinds of things did you do? Were you naughty or nice?

You can add titles, but otherwise your pictures must tell the story. Draw the pictures yourself or print them off the computer, but display them on your paper so that someone looking at it will know what your story is about.

Story Practice: Chicken-free

Tumbleweed the chicken has decided to move house. She has lived with Mrs Perkins in the town for long enough. She dreams of roaming free in the countryside, with the wind in her feathers and only herself for company. She is tired of being surrounded by the other chickens and their constant squawking.

So, one day, while everyone is asleep, Tumbleweed creeps out of the chicken coop and escapes through the fence. She runs along the road, her wings flapping as she picks up speed. At the end of the road she flutter-hops over the gate and into the field. This is it, her freedom begins!

What happens next? Does Tumbleweed really enjoy living on her own in the countryside? Does she miss her chicken friends and Mrs Perkins? Will she go home or live as a free chicken? Or will she be eaten by a hungry fox?

Freestyle

Here are some ideas for you to use in a story or a poem. Make your story or poem as long or as short as you like.

You can decide what happens in it and who your characters are.

Just choose one of the ideas and have a go.

1. Abacus babies

2. Lenny and his tambourine

3. I want to go home!

4. Green scissors

5. Home-made chocolate brownies

6. A crown of silver and gold

7. When we went to the dentist

8. A present for me

9. All I asked for…

10. Carrying the giant jelly

Story Recipe: Sweet little friends

You are going to write a story, but there are some ingredients you need. Follow the instructions below and see what you make in the end.

Ingredients:

22 spiders

1 newspaper

4 pigs

1 hairy jumper

5 packets of sweets

Jumble Words: Scary school

Imagine you have been sent to a new school.

On the first day, you notice things aren't what you expect. There are strange noises in the basement, a girl crying in the hall when there's no one there and your teacher has a bag that moves across the floor by itself.

Using words from the list, put together your story about the scary school. As well as using your own ideas, you should **use at least five of the words** from the list.

Words

Club, plodding, howl, crinkle, furry, web, slimy, banging, scraped, quivers, watching, teeth, shaking, spotty, mouldy, locked, tickled, warts, scratch, thunder, running, rotten, strands, waving, beetles, frost, crows.

Looks familiar...story time

Think of a familiar story, like Snow White or The Wolf and the Three Little Pigs.

Do you have one you like best or know really well? If you're not sure, look at a fairy-tales story book or search fairy-tales online.

Now, **imagine you are in the story.** What would happen? Could you change anything? Or would you just enjoy being part of the adventure?

Before you write your own story, it can be a good idea to write down what happened in the original story. This will help you plan your own story, so you don't forget anything important. This also helps you to decide what to change.

Write a Letter: What's going on?

After your friend moved away, you visited each other every month. When you went there, stayed in their brilliant new tree house. When they came to see you, they had to use the camp-bed from the under-stairs cupboard.

Now your friend isn't answering the phone or replying to emails. You decide to write them a letter and find out what's going on. Are you still friends? Have you done something to upset them? Or are they in trouble and need your help?

Write a letter to your friend, including lots of questions but also reminding them of how long you have been friends and all the fun you had together.

You will need to include **emotions** in this letter, as well as **descriptions** of your friendship.

If you like, you can also write your friend's reply, showing what has happened and whether you can still be friends.

Story Starter: Fingernails!

Mr Green, your new teacher, is as creepy as can be. His eyes seem to change colour when they look at you, his hair blows in the wind when there isn't even a breeze and his fingernails always seem too long.

You and your friends decide to find out what's going on. You go to his house and spy on him. Suddenly, he rushes out, shouting at you. His eyes are blazing bright and his fingernails are longer than ever!

You all run off in different directions, but as the sound fades away you realise you somehow ended up at the back of his back garden where an old forest looms over his fence.

Using at least one of the ideas below, write about what happens next.

Ideas

A bubbling noise

Lots of whispering

Cracking paint

A bright, white light

Friendship

Creaks and groans

Nonsense poem 1

You are going to write a *very short* poem. Here are the rules:

You must have no more than **5 words** on each line

You must have no more than **3 lines** in the whole poem

Your poem should make **no sense** at all! (Sometimes it will make sense by accident!)

Include some of these ideas in your poem, but not all of them.

Ideas

What is your hair like?

How many crumbs on the plate?

Cabbage is good?

The sound of cars

The perfect job

What cats think of mice.

To make it more interesting, don't tell the truth in all your answers!

Example

Here is my poem. See if you can guess which questions I answered.

Yummy, crunchy heads

Too much noise

I'm watching TV

Story Practice: Switched!

You wake up one day and are a different person. You are in someone else's room, in their clothes and, when you look in the mirror, you even look different!

When you go downstairs you find out your family has changed too. Not only do they look different but you seem to have an extra brother.

Just as you are about to start running around, screaming, the phone rings. When you pick it up, your own voice says,

'Don't move, I'm coming round.'

What happens next? Will you solve the mystery of how you

swapped places? Will you get along with your new family? And how will you change back?

Freestyle

Here are some ideas for you to use in a story or a poem. Make your story or poem as long or as short as you like.

You can decide what happens in it and who your characters are.

Just choose one of the ideas and have a go.

1. A rumbly tummy

2. Glowing eyes

3. Over the gate

4. Too many people

5. I can't do it!

6. We played all day

7. Insects and flowers

8. The wrong bus

9. A hundred times

10. Flat cake

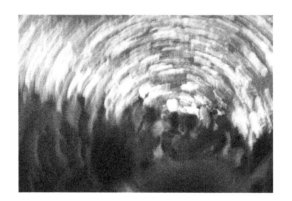

Draw and Write: The best day ever

Draw a picture of the best day you ever had, or of what would be your perfect day. Make sure you include plenty of detail.

Then, in words, explain why this is the best day ever.

You can start by making notes or short sentences, then build up into writing a story about it. Explain what makes it such a special day and why you chose it.

Poetry Line: Ice cream

You are going to write a poem. It doesn't have to rhyme. Each line of the poem should either **start or end with the words shown below**.

Words

flavour, bucket, spoon, chocolate, pudding, grin, melting, ice cream, sprinkles, chocolate, crunchy, delight, fountain, nose

They don't have to be in any order, mix them up if you like. You can also re-use the words, but when you have finished, each word

must have been used at least once. Look at my example to help you.

Example

Sprinkles of pudding

Grin from the spoon

Looks familiar...when I was little

Choose someone you know who is older than you. Now, by asking questions and listening carefully as they talk, find out what they were like as a little child. You might want to make notes while they talk, so that you won't forget anything.

Once they have finished, turn their memories into a story. See how well you can describe them as children. You should try to imagine them as they were then as this will help you make a better story.

Write a letter: OH NO!!!

You are going to write a letter about something horrifying that has just happened. You can't wait to tell someone about it and need to write down everything that took place, before you forget any important details.

Be as descriptive as possible, about your feelings and the event. How do you expect the other person to feel when they read your letter? Will you exaggerate anything, making it seem worse than it was or more exciting?

If you like, include their letter back to you. What did they think?

Do they want more details? Are they horrified? Did you get the reaction you were looking for?

Words

Here are some descriptive words to get you started.

Stunned, shocked, amazed, terrified, petrified, horrified, scared, afraid, fascinated, hypnotised, trembled, excited.

Comic Strip: Aunt Jessie's teeth

Make a story in a comic strip. You can make it as long or as short as you like, but there are three things you need to know to help you:

False teeth come in all shapes and sizes

Aunt Jessie can chew anything

The dog has a funny grin

Freestyle

Choose one or more of the ideas below and use them to write a story or poem. It can be as long or as short as you like.

1. The encyclopaedia of bugs

2. It shivered

3. Baskets for strawberries

4. A shiny place

5. To go to bed

6. The breeze died

7. I will not!

What do you see?

Choose a room and rush into it. As soon as you are in, stop and close your eyes. Turn to the left and open your eyes for 5 seconds. As soon as the 5 seconds are up, run back out of the room.

Now, go and write down what you saw in those 5 seconds. Include as many descriptive words as you can. When you have finished, go back to the room with what you have written and see if you missed anything.

Repeat this exercise in another room but for 10 seconds instead. Compare your writing at the end. Did the extra time make a big difference? Were you surprised at what you could remember?

Poetry Line: Buttercups

You are going to write a poem. It doesn't have to rhyme. Each line of the poem should either **start or end with the words shown below.**

Words

fields, grass, summer, buttercups, gliding, trees, gently, food, calling, birds, path, play, dance, singing, fox, frog, ponies

They don't have to be in any order, mix them up if you like. You can also re-use the words, but when you have finished, each word

must have been used at least once. Look at my example to help you.

Example

Fox runs to play

Calling to the birds

Story Practice: Bags of fun

When Danny buys himself a new school bag, he isn't expecting an adventure. Every time he puts his school things in it, they come back out with the homework done, all his pencils sharpened and his lunch box refilled by the end of school.

Danny is quite happy with this but does wonder what else the bag can do. He borrows his Dad's paperwork from his new project. Dad has been struggling with it for weeks, so if the bag can finish it for him, he's bound to be pleased.

As Danny waits for the bag to work its magic, there is a low rumbling noise and the zip starts to rattle. As he watches, Danny sees light behind the zip and the bag feels very warm.

Scared but desperate to know what is happening, Danny starts to unzip the bag...

What happens next?

Looks familiar...starring

Choose someone you know very well and write down 5 things which would describe them. These can be words, like funny or naughty, or short sentences like, 'loves to bake cakes'.

Example 1

Here is my example for cousin Jane.

Cousin Jane - curly hair, red glasses, likes cats, drives a tiny car, eats chocolate cake, takes me shopping.

Now think of what they would do in one of the **story ideas** below. Pretend they are a character in your story and you can make them do anything.

Ideas

Stuck in a boat in the middle of a lake.

Stealing chickens from the angry farmer.

Going out at night to paint their neighbour's doors a different colour.

Dressing up as a bear and dancing down the street.

Waiting behind bushes and making growling noises.

Now look at my second example where I use what I know about Jane to write a story about her. I have used the story idea of *waiting behind bushes and making growling noises.*

Example 2

Jane was sick of the dogs chasing her cat, Princess. One day, after finishing her cake, Jane went out into her garden and hid behind the hedge. When Toby, the big, scary dog went past, she growled as loud as she could. Toby thought it was another dog so he rushed through the hedge to try and catch it. Jane panicked and ran away. All Toby found was her red glasses, hanging on a branch.

Write a Letter: A special present

It's your birthday and you are excited about all your presents, but there's one you really want to open. For a whole month, the present from your big brother has sat, proudly and mysteriously, in the corner of your bedroom. It's enormous and you had to move a chair to fit it in the room.

Now the big day has arrived and you finally find out what was inside this wonderful-looking present. Your brother is away and you need to write to him, to tell him what you thought of his present.

Decide what the present is and describe it in your letter. You can make your description a mystery still, by describing things *about* the present, without giving away exactly *what* it is.

Was it worth waiting for? Did you feel as excited after opening it as you did before? Are you glad your brother gave it to you?

Choose what sort of **tone** your letter will have: that means, what kind of **feeling** is behind the letter? If you are really pleased with the present, choose words that show how you feel. If you hate it and are feeling disappointed, your letter might be shorter as you won't be able to think of lots of good things to say about the present.

Include lots of description in your letter, describing your feelings as well as the present. You can also include details of your day, what other presents you were given and whether you had a party.

Story Recipe: Tasty moon stew

You are going to write a story, but there are some ingredients you need. Follow the instructions below and see what you make in the end.

Don't be afraid to add extra ingredients if you think your story needs it!

Ingredients:

1 wobbly tooth

2 cups of moonlight

A guinea pig's giggle

4 dandelions

2 hats

Draw and Write: King or Queen for a day

You have won a competition to be treated like a king or queen for a day. Decide what happens on the day but you must be able to boss people about, do whatever you like and spend lots of money!

First draw a picture to show what happens while you are in charge.

When you have drawn your picture, write the story to go with it. Don't forget to mention whether or not you enjoyed the day. Was it what you expected? Or are you happy just being yourself?

Freestyle

Choose one or more of the ideas below and use them to write a story or poem. It can be as long or as short as you like.

1. Freddie gave it two more minutes

2. Tumbling down the hill

3. A clove of garlic

4. When you're ready

5. Whistle what?

6. *A mysterious plant*

7. *In disguise!*

8. *Terrible liars*

9. *The ponies danced*

10. *My hair grew*

Jumble Words: I have to go...

You have to go out for the day with your parents and their friends. You don't want to go as they'll be wandering round shops and you know you'll be bored. To make you feel better, they invite your best friend, Sam.

You and Sam go on the trip but things aren't what you expect. **Using at least five words** from the list below, as well as your own ideas, decide what happens on the bus trip. Where do you go and what happens? Why isn't it what you expected?

Words

Old, rickety, smells, lunch, talking, screams, funny, bendy, butterflies, sunburn, doorways, closed, wink, alarm, drums, badgers, waking, gruesome, free, music, code-words, hiding, pool, hoops, carnivore, creaks, glittering, cackling, supper.

Draw and write: My perfect pet

What is your perfect pet? Do you have one already? What would you like to have in the future?

Draw a picture of your perfect pet and include yourself. This way, you can show how big or small your pet is compared to you. This can be anything at all, from a tiny dog to a giant bear.

Once you have finished the picture, think of a story to go with it. Can you think of an exciting adventure for your pet? Or do they have one already? Make sure you include your pet's name in the story.

A story in pictures: Double trouble

You are going to make a story, using only pictures. In this story, you have to babysit your friend's little brothers.

They are 2 years old and twins. They look cute but as soon as you're left alone, the twins spring into action. They rush all over your house, breaking things and screaming as loud as they can. What can you do to stop them?

You can add titles, but otherwise your pictures must tell the story. Either draw the pictures yourself or print them off the computer, but display them on your paper so that someone looking at it will know what your story is about.

Comic Strip: All at Sea

Make a story in a comic strip. You can make it as long or as short as you like, but there are three things you need to know to help you:

Boats don't row themselves

You're afraid of the water

There's something swimming under the boats

And again...School dinners

First

Write a short poem about school dinners. You can include anything you like, so long as the whole poem is about school dinners.

Try to make each line of the poem **as short as possible**. You could write it, then look at it again and make it shorter the second time.

Then

Look at your poem. What do you need to do to turn it into a story? Should you use longer sentences or perhaps you just need to rearrange it and put your sentences together?

Last

Re-write your poem, turning it into a story. You can add extra words to help it come together, but don't add any extra details to the story. It should be just like your poem, but written in a different way.

Draw and Write: A Space Journey

Imagine what it would be like to be blasted into space then draw a picture and write a story about it.

You can be in a rocket with astronauts, or in a space shuttle as a tourist. Do you stay in space, looking down at the earth? Or do you visit another planet in our solar system? Or a distant planet where no one has ever been?

What do you need to include in the **picture**, to show what is happening in your story? And how will this help you to write your **story**?

Now, write a story about your space journey. Describe the things you have included in your picture and add extra details, such as what the food tasted like, how you felt, what other planets are like and how many aliens you met.

Poetry Line: Birthdays

You are going to write a poem. It doesn't have to rhyme. Each line of the poem should either **start or end with the words shown below**.

Words

Surprise, glimmer, candles, birthday, fun, friends, presents, noise, favourite

They don't have to be in any order, mix them up if you like. You can also re-use the words, but when you have finished, each word

must have been used at least once. Look at my example to help you.

Example

Glimmers of light

Are my favourite

Comic Strip: Tidy up time

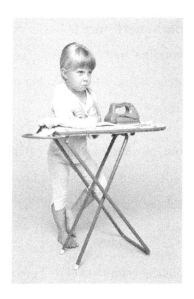

Make a story in a comic strip. You can make it as long or as short as you like, but there are three things you need to know to help you:

You were meant to tidy the whole house

You've spent the day on your computer

Your mother is coming through the door

And again...Octopus

You are going to write a **short story** about an octopus. You can include any details you like, make it exciting, scary or even your pet! The story only needs to be a few lines but make sure plenty of things happen in it.

Now, go back and look at what you have written. Write it out again, putting each full sentence on its own line. Then, look at your sentences and take out any words that aren't important, like 'and', 'if', 'but', then'.

Now, write your sentences again, making them **much shorter**. They should still have their own lines. When you have finished, read it out loud. You have created a **poem** from your own story. Change anything else you think you need to and admire your work!

Jumble Words: Time snap

It seemed like a normal gate when you first saw it. You climbed over to get into the field, because you couldn't open the gate. Halfway over, there was a terrible cracking sound and the gate fell apart, leaving only a couple of pieces of wood still in place.

As you lay on the ground, looking at what you had done, a sound came from behind you.

Now, seconds after breaking the gate and hearing the sound, you find yourself rushing through the air, colours around you, wind blowing through your hair. You land with a thud, back in the field. But now the grass is long and there are cows. The gate is back where it was, but is new.

You have travelled back in time! How far did you come? What is the year? What happens next? And how do you find your way home?

Using some of the words below, write a story about your adventures in the past. Use at least **five words** from the list.

Found, terrible, grassy, fuel, victory, clumsy, gold, eyebrows, cap, freckles, whined, pouring, fried, tiny, corn, cobbles, tractor, flowers, ponies, stream, rescue, bakery, pinafore, clatter, moonlight, tremendous, mouse, water wheel, soldiers, key, window, trepidation, sneaking, music, workhouse, treasure, joy.

Story Recipe: Snowy surprise

You are going to write a story, but there are some ingredients you need. Follow the instructions below and see what you make in the end.

Ingredients

1 small present

2 popping noises

4 exclamation marks!

2 hot dinners

3 tubes of marshmallow paste

1 small icicle

A little boat to mix them in

Nonsense poem 2

You are going to write a very short poem. Here are the rules:

You must have no more than **5 words** on each line

You must have no more than **3 lines** in the whole poem

Your poem should make **no sense** at all! (Sometimes it will make sense by accident!)

Ideas

Include some of these ideas in your poem, but not all of them.

What do you think of porridge?

How many bees are in the world?

Where does smoke come from?

What happens when you stub your toe?

How long should you hide?

What is that smell?

To make it more interesting, don't tell the truth in all your answers!

Example

Here is my poem. See if you can guess which questions I answered.

Ooh, ooh, ah!

I'll wait forever,

Sticky and sad

A story in pictures: Pet store disaster

You are going to make a story, using only pictures. In this story, you get locked in the pet store. You don't realise until the lights are turned off. No one knows you are there so you must find a way to escape. Using only what you can find in the pet store, work out how you would break out.

You can add titles, but otherwise your pictures must tell the story. Either draw the pictures yourself or print them off the computer, but display them on your paper so that someone looking at it will know what your story is about.

What do you see?

It can be hard to think of what to include in a story so this time you are going to practice turning real-life descriptions into story descriptions. You don't have to think of anything that is not real, you just have to change it a little to make it sound more like a story.

Paragraph first

You are going to write a short, descriptive paragraph based on what you see around you. To make it more difficult, close your eyes, turn around and face a different direction. Now, open your eyes and write down what you see.

Story second

Once you have finished your paragraph, read it through and see how you can change it to make it into a story. What would you need to write differently?

Look at my example to help you.

Example

The table is covered in papers from the mail, some opened and some not. There is a kettle nearby and a bread bin. The kettle is starting to boil.

This might become: *The table was covered with heaps of letters, piling on top of each other. They were like a small mountain, with white paper instead of snow.*

or

The kettle boiled, rattling on the table top, ready for the tea. Should she read the letters now? No, tea first, letters later.

Story Starter: Neighbours

There is an old, broken down house near where you live. It's been empty for years and no one can remember who used to live there.

Now it's starting to change and you see lights on in the windows, the garden growing tidier, the front door is painted and the chimney has been fixed. But you never see anyone there.

Using one or more of the ideas below, write about what happens with the house. It can be anything you like, but you must include one of these ideas in a way that makes sense within the story.

Ideas

An old, brown truck

Too many windows

A face behind the door

A pink dress, blowing in the wind.

*Blossoming trees in wi*nter.

You can use more than one idea, if you like.

Poetry Line: Building Site

You are going to write a poem. It doesn't have to rhyme. Each line of the poem should either **start or end with the words shown below.**

Words

spade, bricks, shouting, sun, drilling, building, laughter, music, hammer, castle, house, treehouse, cottage, tumbles, bucket, singing, mixing, making, painting, fixing, windows, doors, key.

They don't have to be in any order, mix them up if you like. You can also re-use the words, but when you have finished, each word must have been used at least once. Look at my example to help you.

Example

Shouting in the treehouse

Tumbles from the doors.

And again...the advert

First

You are going to star in an advert for burgers. You have to eat a burger and pretend it tastes great while a camera films you. Write a short story about what happens.

Think about whether you enjoy it and if it was your choice to do it. Do you like burgers? Or do you hate them, now you've had to eat them all day?

Then

When you finish, write the story out again but this time from the point of view of the **camera person**. What do they think of the advert? Are they tired of burgers too? Do they think you did a good job? Would they like to be acting instead of filming?

Last

When you have finished, read your two stories again and see how the same day looks different in each one.

Write a Letter: I hate you!

Someone has done something horrible to you and now you are really angry with them. They used to be one of your favourite people too!

Write them a letter to let them know how you feel. Can you ever forgive them? Will you mention in the letter what they did to make you hate them? Or will it be a mystery?

Make your letter at least three paragraphs long with plenty of emotions in it.

Comic Strip: Beans!

Make a story in a comic strip. You can make it as long or as short as you like, but there are three things you need to know to help you:

Not all beans grow into beanstalks

You sell your laptop for a bag of beans

Beans don't usually have little feet

What do you see?

You are going to write a short poem using only what you see around you but this time try to write **in detail** about one item, instead of describing a room full at a time.

So if you are outside, you can describe big things like a building or a truck. If you are at home, you could describe things like the TV, an ornament or a picture.

Example

Here is my poem. Notice how short it is and that it doesn't rhyme:

Small, fat cat

Snores on my skirt

One white foot, raised

Like a queen

As she purrs.

Write a letter: To yourself

Something a little different this time. You are going to write a letter to your **future self**. When you have finished, it will be sealed away, not to be opened until you are much older.

What would you like to put in the letter? Will you include lots of details of what your life is like, in case you forget when you're older? Or will you say what you hope to be like in the future?

This one is completely up to you; just remember you are writing it to yourself, from now to the future.

Nonsense poem 3

You are going to write a very short poem. Here are the rules:

You must have no more than **5 words** on each line

You must have no more than **3 lines** in the whole poem

Your poem should make **no sense** at all! (Sometimes it will make sense by accident!).

Ideas

Include some of these things in your poem, but not all of them.

What was the song you sang?

How old are your brothers or sisters?

Who would you like to meet?

What would you do if you could fly?

What do you think about going to the dentist?

To make it more interesting, don't tell the truth in all your answers!

Example

Here is my poem. See if you can guess which questions I answered.

I'd fall into the sky

To meet the golden fish

Too many jabs though

Story Recipe: A Snow Globe Surprise

You are going to write a story using the ingredients below. What do you make in the end?

Ingredients:

Half a cup of strawberry mousse

12 snowflakes

1 piece of rock

3 locks of hair

1 chance to get it right

Freestyle

Choose one or more of the ideas below and use them to write a story or poem. It can be as long or as short as you like.

1. Yes, please!

2. Turning to see

3. The stream bubbled

4. Porcupines are lazy

5. I want out!

6. *Cream and sugar*

7. *I couldn't get it back*

8. *Grandma's toes*

9. *Sunshine in my eyes*

10. *A blaze of colour*

Ready for more?

If you would like more creative writing ideas, visit
www.amandajharrington.co.uk or http://freebrians.blogspot.co.uk for news
of creative writing courses and free resources.

You might also like:

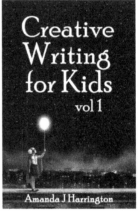

54683023R00098

Made in the USA
Columbia, SC
04 April 2019